Things We Don't Know
We Don't Know

Things We Don't Know We Don't Know

Matt Mason

The Backwaters Press

Also by Matt Mason:

Mistranslating Neruda, New Michigan Press, 2003
When the Bough Breaks, Lone Willow Press, 2005

Cover photo by John Spence © 2006 John Spence. Used by permission.

Author photo by Sarah McKinstry-Brown © 2006 Sara McKinstry-Brown.

Cover design by Bristol Creative.

Book design by Greg Kosmicki.

Proofreading by Aaron Anstett.

Published by: The Backwaters Press
                    Greg Kosmicki, Editor/Publisher
                    Rich Wyatt, Editor
                    3502 N. 52nd St.
                    Omaha, NE 68104-3506
                    www.thebackwaterspress.homestead.com
                    gkosmicki@cox.net

                ISBN: 0-9765231-8-3

Acknowledgments

I'd like to thank the following publications for including poems from this collection:

Bovine Free Wyoming: "The Swedish Turnip"
Berkeley Poetry Review: "Navigation"
Central Avenue: "Untitled Poem For Sarah," "The Revolution Will Not Be Written"
Chiron Review: "Teaching"
Ellipses: "Frontier Days"
From Page to Stage and Back Again (anthology by Wordsmith Press): "Code Orange"
The Great American Road Show (anthology from Logan House Press): "Coffee and Astronomy," "The Good News"
Green Mountain Review: "The Funny Poet Renounces Funny Poetry And Concentrates On Making The World A Better, More Beautiful Place (In Which He Has Sex More Often)"
IdioM: "After the 1996 Fiesta Bowl"
Laurel Review: "Midnight Train to Omaha"
Literal Latté: "I May Not Know Where I'm Going But I'm Making Damn Good Time"
Maelstrom: "Snack Cakes"
Mississippi Review, (online edition): "Code Orange"
Omaha Pulp: "The 1,001 Loads of Laundry"
Poet Lore: "The Good News"
Prairie Schooner: "Morning Song"
Research File (a program of Radio Nederlands:Wereldomroep): "Science and Love"
Santa Clara Review: "Ode to Marlin Perkins"
Wisconsin Review: "The Thin Line of What I Know"

Some of these poems also appeared in the Morpo Press chapbooks *Coffee and Astronomy and Other Poems,* and *Red, White, Blue.*

This collection is dedicated to those friends, teachers, family members, and barely-known folks in poetry reading crowds who've encouraged and assisted me: especially Sarah who counts as a little of every one of those categories. I am indebted to each one of you (though you still have to buy your own copies of the book, sorry).

Contents

I come to writing this foreword wanting to tell you what an entertaining writer Matt Mason is. But now I read how Matt Mason doesn't want to be a "funny poet" anymore—or so he tells us in one of these wonderful poems. I don't think he really has a choice, though. The blessing may sometimes seem like a curse, but he cannot help it. He's funny. He may want to renounce the cow poems that earned him the love of expatriate Nebraskans everywhere, but he cannot help but to look at our world with open eyes, and so how can he not help but notice how strange and (darkly) funny our world has become with its John Ashcroft Remixes, its Rumsfeldian empty rationalizations of war, and its elaborately color-coded and accessorized levels of alarm and paranoia.

But let's not make the mistake of believing that being "funny" isn't serious. I think it's essential to the national dialogue. In fact, if after the next all-too-predictable State of the Union Address, and after the opposing party's equally predictable retort, there happened to be a place in the program for the Poet's Response, I'd want Matt Mason to deliver it. Because unlike the marketing clones of our culture, I could depend on him *not* to be predictable.

Instead, he would be smart and tender and funny all at once. He'd speak in his own voice and it'd sound like no one else's. He might begin to tell us, as he does in these poems, about the true meaning of the grave of Elvis, or how he left God hanging forgotten in a closet. He might describe the temples erected to Marlin Perkins in "deepest Omaha." He might even tell you how you might even find your own personal Jesus, one who not only saves but recycles. Listening to him, we'd be surprised. At first it might seem weird. We might mistakenly believe that he was just being "funny." But when he'd finished talking we'd finally understand that his gift (and our gift) in being "funny" is a deeply political act—especially now, in a country where the happy surprises of our lives are contrary to the business plan and, in some states, pretty damn near against the law.

— Ron Block

She's alone at a table for four at the bookstore coffee shop,

> same as me,

and our eyes meet and I think

> "It's too bad I'm a screwup," and I think

"Maybe I could straighten out if it meant I could kiss her,"

> as she sits like a book I just need to read, two of us

taking up eight spaces across this place;

> we could conserve and share,

"Think Globally, Act Locally,"

> sit at the same table in polite mystery of one another,

shower together to save water

> but I don't know if she cares

about water conservation,

> I can only tell that her hair falls like rain,

she has more fashion sense than I do, our eyes meet

> and I'm scared of her,

all her *Noes*,

> all her *Yeses,*

her *I want to have a babys,*

> her eyes

as small as stars,

> the light having taken years to reach me here

at this gargantuan table as big as my life.

Iowa flows across the windshield
like a relaxation video; I turn off the radio and listen
to wind rattle the window near my cheek.
Gravel scattered after the last ice popping
in the wheel wells, I daydream about being in Des Moines
already, with you.
The familiar mile-markers pass like hand-holds up a cliff:
Number 31, and Six-Eighty becomes I-Eighty;
    66, I'm halfway to Des Moines; 88,
            two-thirds; 99, three-fourths; 121, eleven-twelfths...

At number 60, the Purple Martin Train lounges, a primped wreck, zig-
zagging and only a little purple.
On one trip, I stopped
and bought an "It's Purple Martin Time!" button at the caboose-
made-museum. I only stopped there once;
like I only had one flat sandwich at 4-Sons; only made one trip
up the stairs of the observation tower near the Beebeetown exit,
  one look from above at the little crease of interstate,
    the thin line of what I know
        among all the foreign fields and hills
            stretching from it like butterfly wings.

I always mean to follow some of the signs,
detour through someplace
like Persia, Casey, Atlantic, Van Meter, Waukee, Prairie Rose State Park,
all just tin signs and exits to me.
I never go further off the interstate
than the Have A Nice Day water tower smiling from Adair,
never go past the gas stations,
never put my fingers
to the skin of the East
or West Nishnabotna Rivers;
never slow at mile 71,
  where that pond, always flat and still no matter how windy,
    stretches two drowning elms like bony arms
          clinging onto the sky.

As the counties slowly metamorphose
from Pottawattamie to Polk, I watch the trees along the road perform
all their acts: fat, naked, flowering, flaming, green, chainsawed.
I know the corn by name,
fast-motion life flowing from conception by John Deeres
through green puberty, then fading,
then death at the teeth of their own creators;
  the bodies removed, their ground left for crows and cows
          to tidy and fertilize.

More of you forms
as the white-on-green numbers count upward.
At 14, I see your feet; at 23,
you have hands, a hazy middle, lips;
by 57 or 58, you are female; 85, your eyes
  are grey like the sky; 96, the cornfields fade
          into your hair. I know every mile ticking by, I know, can drive
                  by sense of touch.

We'll start with a week of seconds
and won't sleep,
except for pure enjoyment, our bodies
touching like shut scissors.
We'll know each crumb we taste,
luxuriate in every calorie,
in the sparkle and crack
of every second.

In the week of minutes,
we'll love how grass feels
and have really good pizza
and drive to Yosemite, talking
around the songs on the radio
and my Van Morrison tape. There
will be something extra-delightful
about the taste of pineapple
in the week of minutes.

We'll skip the week of hours,
going, instead, to the week of days;
because we
will not be predictable,
especially inside poems.

When the week of days comes,
we'll read to each other and make love,
then like the romance so much, we'll
walk in the mostly-dark and make
new names for constellations
that someone else just happened to
be lucky enough to see
before us. In this week—and
this is important—we'll find
we need new words.

When the week of weeks comes,
we'll wonder what comes next:
a week of months? fortnights?
decades? the missing week
of hours? Will daylight savings
affect it? Will it just be a week
free of cute conceits, or
will no week be able to follow,
will this be the end-all week
where God comes down—
well, not God, but someone from
God's staff—and hands us
a phonebook-sized stack of papers,
asks us to rate all of creation
on a scale of 1 to 5?

We eat French fries at each other in Lyons, nothing more
to say, I'm tired of talking about the ex-girlfriend in all my poems;
maybe she does this on purpose, maybe she calls and
says she still loves me, she feels sad, so that she never has to leave
the poems. Maybe I love her, maybe I want her
in my apartment instead of in Portland. Cooking
with my stove and pans, watching TV in the next room,
brushing her teeth at my sink, sleeping next to me.

We live far enough apart
that her midnight is my 2 a.m., all of Rocky Mountain
Time exists between us, an hour neither of us knows;
maybe someday we'll see it, realize that she's an hour
slow, and I'm an hour fast, that we could meet in Pueblo
or Albuquerque and find some solar harmony between us.
Despite what Mr. Einstein might say to this,
I've done stupider things

and seen them work. I've put kiwifruit into pancake batter, gone
into debt studying poetry, bet on the Minnesota Vikings,
driven two-hundred miles for a decent donut. God gets bored sometimes
and rewards creative idiocy; hell, any idiocy,
as God'd probably be the first to admit
how dull order can be. What else explains
Satan? Nixon? Poets
writing sestinas about cows?

But what can I say as I dip another French fry into ranch dressing,
what else? Six months ago, if she'd made this
phone call six months ago, I might be having sex
instead of writing this poem, I might be at Lake Tahoe
instead of Lyons. I might. I might
have been kidnapped by mutant lunar llamas;
what might ain't. This planet has no time zone where clocks run
six months behind mine. And even if there was,

I wouldn't be able to afford the long-
distance charges. I wouldn't be able to call
myself there, anyway. I'd only go broke on a minute with my answering
          machine:
Hello, I'm not able to come to the phone right now,
when I'm re-abled to use the phone, I'll call you
barring some random act of dis-abling...
What would I even say to myself? Would I say, "Hold on!"
"Let go!" "Change your damned message!" Or would I call

her, tell her I'm in February
and it's raining
and she loves me again
and isn't that wild?
Six months. What's
actually changed, then? When
did time translate into distance
and distance to volume?

Why do I keep shoving
fries into my mouth, trying
to find the one bit of deep-
fried potato shrapnel that finally satisfies?
Why talk, write poems, make love, eat, stare expectantly as if
this one time, God will look up
from His French fries, clear that windy throat,
and do more than fucking smile?

Ode to Marlin Perkins

I remember sitting in the cold
Hawaiian hotel room,
watching as a plastic anchorman
labeled the world's troubles
and dropped them in my lap.
And at the top of this pile lay Marlin Perkins,
dead at seventy-one.

When people learn where I'm from,
they smugly ask:
"How is Marlin Perkins?"
And I tell them
he's dead.
In their embarrassment, they whisper:
"I'm sorry,
I didn't know."

His polar bear hair
and calm control
in the clutch of anacondas
made him more than mortal
in his Sunday evening searches
to capture pygmy antelope,
cage Bulgarian battle rabbits,
catch Northern snow gators,
and completely captivate me
until the last Alaskan lemur
was tranquilized.

As I drive past the temple-like structure
standing among the gargantuan hills of steel and stone
in deepest Omaha,
I see the proud Indian head
like an icon carved into a mountainside
and wonder
if Marlin's soul rests there.

How can it be,
I now find his undead image
smiling like a lion
in my living room?
He's rounding up rabid kangaroo
and isn't gone, for the gods
of syndication (and his assistant, Jim)
have brought him back to me.
Marlin has wrestled free
from the suckered tentacle of Death,
and I pray to him!

Rutabaga;
now that's a word I always enjoyed. Root
a bay guh. I used to know a girl
who reminded me of a rutabaga. This, of course,
was long before I looked
it up inside the *World
Book*. The *World Book* kills
all romance. If it had been correct,
she would've had a bulbous body
curving to hair that stuck in all directions like demented antennae.
She didn't.
I didn't know a rutabaga was actually a turnip;
she was no turnip.
Her posture was far too good.
I think she's engaged
to a pilot now.
Too bad, because I probably still love her.
I read some Vonnegut for answers,
but he just said, "So it goes."
This does not help.
And I find it hard to tell
someone that there's a rutabaga
rooted deep inside me
long past any reasonable harvest.

It is in us somewhere, if only in the chipped ringlets of a fingernail: the maple, the eucalyptus, those crooked little bushes that lead us to forsake that damned formica paneling and lay down solid, processed oak on our counters as the primeval brain within us screeches and tries to recall the feel of branches in paws, winds and leaves stroking and scratching fur as we pull ourselves upward, inward and bare yellowed teeth at the dirt. So we bend ourselves onto the counter, open the cabinet and push aside the soup, the flour, the paprika, and climb inside: baring our teeth at the linoleum below, not minding the maple syrup bottle pushing into spine, close the dark, brown door and feel like Jesus, so much pain to finally be rejoined with wood.

Damn you parents who will not admit it! You give your own child plastic blocks to build with. You should not, then, be surprised when little Matthew has his first divorce or abuses drugs or starts fires or appears naked on bus routes or becomes a poet crying out from some deep grove of his soul for real Lincoln Logs, for Tinker Toys, for blocks of firm, painted wood.

(The Dutch folk dancers may have splinters in their feet
but I can feel their ecstasy.)

The blue flame pours impotently down the rock logs, sparking no desire to rip off all clothing and feel the hot glow everywhere on our bodies, no frenzy of whirling in a circle of flaming sequoia to the call of fist pounding animal skin stretched over a screaming mouth of wood.

There isn't that joy in watching an entire floor of carpeting, an entire condominium burn, though cigarettes and caffeine can tranquilize the part of our brain that remembers best, that remembers, that remembers wood.

Children in Hell
probably recite multiplication tables,
hold spelling bees, and eat meatloaf
just like I did.

Though they learn the alphabet by chanting,
The quick, brown fox
jumps over the lazy God
and they never have summer vacation.

Maybe I will drink hot bleach
and be hired there.
I could teach History:
the Wild West, maybe.

I could talk about Sitting Bull and Black Elk
on stage with Buffalo Bill's Wild West Show.
Chief Joseph reciting,
From where the Sun now stands,

I will fight no more, forever,
twice daily to a spotlight,
shouts, hoots, and the smell
of sweat and cigarettes.

I will ask my class,
Did the frozen souls of ghost dancers
warm by a fire, eat roasted papa somewhere;
or did they melt in slow drops,

returning to the earth, whispering up at our feet?
as if I know the answer.
I don't. But maybe one of my students will.
And I won't feel so much

like a lumberjack at sea
with nothing to hack
but my sails, my oars,
the planks along the bottom.

Badlands: December, 1890

> *So the thunder beings shot off all their bolts...The forests were set on fire, and flames consumed everything except the top of the rock on which the humans had taken refuge...The earth glowed red-hot, and Unktehi, big and small, burned up and died, leaving only their dried bones in the Mako Sicha, the Badlands...*
>
> —Lame Deer, from "Wakinyan Tanka, The Great Thunderbird"

These bones,
though bones still, feel boldness again; they arch up
to shove against the sky; they finally see those who dried them and dropped
*   them onto the dust*
flee and howl as they once did.

Children of blood drip
up the ribs, ripping a thin path through the snow, hoping to find
a pass across these bleached reminders
of the long-ago mercy of gods

before their pursuers overtake them.
The Lakotas' breath
spills in thick clouds,
then disappears into the overwhelming black.

And there, high on the spine,
they finally look over to see the cracks and
pits and small bones
of the south slope.

And on that pass,
they join hands and dance,
spinning like a hoop, like a second hand
while the hour hand struggles to stay still.

A child wanders from the throbbing drum
and sits high in the eye socket of a skull.
She sleeps. She sees the clouds so much thicker
than they will ever be again:

She sees lightning falling
short of the earth,
hears thunder shout in hollow syllables.
She watches rain spill into ice

as the clouds sweep
west, leaving
just a smudge of small fires
across the sky.

And these bones never again fear thunder,
never again fear gods or spirits
or saviors. The children of blood dance
and shriek for hope,

not seeing how the ground cracks
open into graves,
not feeling the blood
freeze over their skin.

Night in the Shenandoah River Valley

The sun yawns low and red over the valley where
Stonewall Jackson didn't care that
he was outnumbered by a sea of damp blue uniforms.
After the sun gave way to coalsmoke black, Stonewall Jackson
must have lain in his tent, wondering what surrounded him,
what birds or bugs out there make that droning song
washing in and out till dawn.

And the next morning, did he dress sharp as a saber and
stand on the Blue Ridge like a tourist,
thinking about bringing his family here, having a picnic
before getting back to the business of making valleys bleed?

Trees have come and gone since then,
and farms and homesteads, too many wildflowers to count
(though the effort wouldn't be a waste).
And I lie here listening,
wondering how many weary dreams
have lain themselves to sleep in this same place.

Ode to a Confederate Flag

Stonewall Jackson kicked some ass
until his own confused men blasted away
at his shadows and flesh. That's the easy part:
letting go of your new wife
to shoulder an old hunting rifle and a pack of warm cornbread
and walking to town,
that's easy.
Yes, thousands of ruptured men stiffening in pastures
is easy, blood and grey matter, the crackle of your own bone and gristle,
the stuff of destruction;

as no matter how hard General Jackson hammered
he couldn't make one goddamned pumpkin blossom.

In some revolutions, they still throw poems
with the explosives, can you believe that?
That while I've been mixing poetry
about how painful it is to be middle class and white
and so misunderstood,
that in some revolutions, they still throw
poems with the explosives,
not funny little anecdotes, not cute little pornography,
not nothing little about it as little don't kill
the tiger, little don't make a free press a danger,
little don't draw blood from a tyrant.
And that's what they still do
in some revolutions.
They crowd around tables
made from doors or boxes, they whisper
their cocktails, stir
verbs in one jar, nouns in another, hook up a timer,
and sweat. Most nursery rhymes, you know,
were bold as free blood,
those "London Bridges," those butchers, bakers,
candlestick makers knew more
about experience than my lovesick quatrains,
my grape haikus, my training wheels and ice cream,
they would've looked to a time like this
and written words that would not leave
a single house standing.

Gregory Corso got such rave reviews.
Not his latest book, I'm talking other news:
he spent fifty years writing, but it's the one day dead
that got his fame in all the papers, that gets his name read

because poets don't make the covers of *Entertainment Weekly*,
they make page 16, they make obituaries.
So you won't see William Kloefkorn in a book review section
unless he writes a review of a Jackie Collins collection,

as they teach the same rules at all the journalism schools:
Don't mention a book of poems till they pull the body from a pool.
They'll write, "That touchdown was poetry" or "Travolta was poetic,"
but the writers never rock out to a Billy Collins lyric.

See, Sylvia and Dylan knew how to get some coverage,
drink yourself to death or stick your head in an oven;
Berryman, Jarrell, Sexton, and Crane
knew the final step on their walks of fame

wouldn't be box office bonanzas or talk show popularity:
the way a poet makes *People* is posthumously.
So let the latest network idols, athletes and musicians
flash their retouched teeth across the grocery-line editions;

don't worry who's dating Britney or dragging Oprah through the mud,
if you choose to write poems, you choose to write with blood
because poets don't make the covers of *Entertainment Weekly*,
they make page 16, they make obituaries.

I

And in the Central Valley,
some of the kiwifruit aren't round
in an eggish way, but look like
Siamese twins and triplets neatly made
into one kiwi, like fur-
wrapped Alaskans pressed together to stay warm,
small commemorative figurines of Mount Rushmore
with presidential faces seriously unshaven. Just as green
inside as the accepted kiwi, the same
wave of seeds in rolling connect-the-dots smiles,
just as sweet, just as potent
in tenderizing tongues if you eat too many
or chew too long.

But you don't see these in grocery stores.
They don't fit precisely
through the machines that sort.

II

The kiwi I just bought
was nearly perfect,
deserving at least a line or two here
both praising and eulogizing its firmness, flavor,
roundness, largeness, vitamin content, even though
it grew up in New Zealand, not California.

III

California is where I found them
lovely. On eating one last autumn, I felt amazement,
as if the Holy Grail of fruit had always been
just a market trip away;

I immediately made a friend promise
to remind me someday that kiwifruit is fantastic
and should be eaten.

I forget things like that.

IV

They really don't seem so sexual
to me, as some friends say they are:

in some ways, the skin reminding them
of the pubic area on a woman;
some say they hang in plastic produce sacks
like testicles. But I
am too fascinated with my own sexual denials, so
in this realm I must ask you
to use your own imagination
rather than borrowing mine.

V

But then there are those wonderful,
bulbous, large, irregular kiwi
(remember them from section one?):

I can almost see those doorknockers
clogging up the automatons, refusing to pass
down the neatlittle holes, only sold at farmer's markets
in Davis, California or Hokitika, New Zealand
near where they grow, accepted
and cherished by the warm palms of poets
who write odes to them
as an important matter of taste.

And those uncorrected papers I was supposed to hand back yesterday
follow me like shadows needing commas. They're here,
always with me like Run-On Sentence Jesus;
they're here in my dreams; in my backpack; in
my underwear drawer; they're in the Sports section of my morning paper;
falling from the trees in Fontenelle Forest; inside
pumpkins; on the radio at the top of every hour;
riding broomsticks in front of the moon; rolling in
from the river as evening spills; spelled out
by marching bands at halftimes of televised football games
in awkward, wordy formations
that would flow so much smoother if you'd cut out that drum section and that
        trombonist and add a few tubas
for clarity and balance.

I'd take a break, run away, even
risk driving through a snowstorm to Memphis or Grand Forks,
but the road, the road
signs scare me. All those Stuckey's billboards, truck stop menus,
little towns in Iowa;
and worse, those
huge pen-strokes of concrete
that climb up hills and run beside rivers
in miles-long proofreading errors.

On The $17 "Platinum" Tour

Poorboys and Pilgrims with families
And we are going to Graceland

—from "Graceland" by Paul Simon

And maybe it wouldn't be so bad
if he hadn't died in the 70s.

Even the awfullest, most snivelingest European frogprince
left a noble tourist attraction just by getting lynched by peasants

in the right century:
eventually a tourist board evolved

who bought what stones were left, restacked them,
there is no green shag carpet on the ceiling,

no mirrored walls reflecting an eternity
of baby blue, no fourteen television sets,

suede sheets, gold sinks,
tiger-pattern bell-bottom jumpsuits.

It took a day-and-a-half to drive here from Nebraska,
over the river to Iowa, deep into Missouri, past the Branson billboards of
         celebrities we didn't know were still alive,

into Arkansas, where even the Klan chips in to adopt a highway,
places it seems we should need passports to see,

on through the rusting Ozarks,
where it was so close to Thanksgiving that the yard-chickens

were still looking for the yard-turkey,
and across the Mississippi.

After such a drive,
legs unfolding with difficulty, breath stale from potato chips and Diet Pepsi,

I stood, hoping
for a headache to pass,

expecting catharsis, expecting
climax to tidal wave at any second.

Priscilla droned on about his dinner buddies, the Aztec Sun
was stuffed with a department store mannequin, the cheapest

souvenir keychains still cost three bucks, and the house looked like my house
would've looked like if my parents'd had more cash than God to play with;

and the workers stationed everywhere
didn't seem like those Disney flunkies with dustpan in hand,

smile screwed on solely to avoid being fired:
these workers,

six o'clock on a November night, bird almost thawed at home for tomorrow,
these workers joked and smiled despite eight hours

of those damned Christmas ballads, pacing their little post by an
        ordinary-looking kitchen that people keep paying to see,
and there they are, looking fulfilled so long as no one uses flash photography
        in the racquetball court.

By the end,
in the carnival lights at the gravesite, my

hands were twitchy, my head
throbbing as if loaded with a cold railroad spike:

all our hips were still, our wallets light, no ghosts or aliens or two-headed love
        chillun appeared in the fountain.
And everything under this ground

could be suited up
in gold and platinum but still couldn't breathe in

this smell of spices, sauce, and pork ribs
hanging low over Memphis tonight.

There are some kisses you will not forget.
You will be able to recall perfectly
the strain in your left thigh
from sitting that way to face her across the couch.
You could be standing in a McDonald's somewhere
and still picture the dimness, a little light from her kitchen
in a rectangle over on the floor, the triangles
in the yellow quilt over her legs,
her closed eyes, the slouch of her head.
When more than her whole body responds, you
have done something irreparable.

I left God in a closet back in Denver.
But like a good son, I miss
mom more. I suppose, though,
she'll eventually have sheets to put away
and she'll open the closet door,
not noticing Him at first, then gasping,
when she recognizes Him folded over a hanger.
She'll say quickly
she has a careless son who just forgot Him
and she'd better roll Him up and mail Him. But
she'll know better really.
She'll take Him upstairs and make Him
some soup, not mention anything
directly, but ask my sister
to pry a little:
   do I hang out in atheist bars now;
    is it something John Paul said;
   when I call, will I ask about Him,
   will I ever want to talk to Him;
   did He always eat this much and use
   so many towels?

The Lord took him outside and said:
"Look at the sky and try to count the stars;
you will have as many descendants as that."

—Genesis 15:5

My muse's name is "Eliezar"
or "Elvis" or something like that; he mutters,
"Ya don't want babies, baby," and that's okay
by me, but it might upset the girl I love,
I admit—and I should know, having taken dozens of
showers on this—I've never really felt a parental calling.

If anything, the opposite. My muse sings,
"Give unto me a car, give unto me a road."
Maybe throw in a Triple-A atlas and a tent
and a couple bucks for gas: zip the black sky shut over my
face, poke out some stars with a ballpoint, and, hidden
underneath, I'll keep myself immortal with dreams.

What I don't want is to
feel like a "love stinks" poster child again,
imagining a telethon or letter campaign to
get me laid. When I feel uneasy like this, reflex
reaches for a backpack and traveller's checks,
except I'm out of cash,

crash-landed and making résumés,
and I need a shower or a journey
or a dream or maybe to make love again, pull
her over me and hold her as if
I could make her into moonlight that shows everything
more mystically, slower.

But the best I can find tonight is refrigerator light,
that shows everything
too bright, giving the illusion of cold
calm, as if nothing is slowly molding or souring,
as if everything stays okay if
observed in the right wattage.

Whose voice called me deep
into Belgium anyway? Did it speak from
my brother's photographs, the brief
comments in *Let's Go,* an ex-girlfriend

with Belgian roots, a poster of Flemish cows
mooing like mythical sirens, wind under a full moon murmuring
broooooosh, or just a fascination
with running and recklessness?

And nothing at all
wanted to work neatly: trains moved slower than expected, rail
schedules acted surly, I needed to change trains and
train stations in Paris when I only know enough

French to order pan au chocolat or find a toilet. So I wandered
through the station in indecision, snapping
at panhandlers, quick to whisper death-
threats at train-schedule machines. Suddenly

I was madly hopping
whatever train might take me
Bruggeward, sitting on a train to Bruxelles
with an unused ticket to Lille in my pack, picturing Don Quixote

sighing approvingly.
And I made Brugge by twilight
after a whole day on trains, my mind planning
one fast night to look around, then more

trains in the morning. Unaware
that in half-an-hour, autumn flowers would bloom
in my eyes, that an hour more would have me declare
to miss the next day's ferry for Ireland (then change

my mind, then again,
then consider it under a hot shower,
then change again
and again).

And why not leave in the morning?
See Brugge only at sunset and sunrise, in illumination dim
and romantic like candlelight, like a passing face I'll always
half-remember as the most beautiful and perfect on this earth?

The canals with leaves spread across them like embers
spilled over an ebony table; lamplight
shining on Madonna and Child statuettes set
into building corners above cobblestone streets;

dark but welcoming alleyways; joined
houses with high, sharp
foreheads; the sound of horse hooves striking
one street over:

all Flemish paintings for my thoughts
to frame and revisit even more
than those galleries of Prague and Paris
where it rains, where dogs shit on the sidewalk, where trees are only green.

I set my alarm
then decided not to turn it on. I slept through sunrise,
missed my train, my boat, I will stay
this time, I will

be rained on, feel
my feet ache, pay way too much for a Diet Coke.
I want to actually understand who you are.
I want to finally get past only loving you.

After the 1996 Fiesta Bowl

One guy jumps out of a car and strips
to red briefs, swinging his pants
around his head and howling; the face-painted guys
jump off the pickup to

trade high-fives in traffic, a champagne bottle
gets handed out a Buick window, horns a-honkin',
red people running around cars and steaming
on a January midnight.

Cops on horseback wade through the red flags, above
even the hooting wildheads riding
on someone's shoulders like big-ass Jesus on Saint Christopher's back
braying "Go Big Red" with a few thousand of their closest buds;

cops guard the traffic signs so they won't become souvenirs:
some lean against squad cars
kinda smiling, some visibly tired and on overtime.
We scream and flow,

take pictures, hug, throw beer cans, climb light posts, slap hands,
greet, grunt, and though we are Nebraskans and so keep most of our clothes
          on, we do
think wildly that if all of Omaha gets naked
what can they do?

My fingers stiffen like garden hose
but we all keep slapping and celebrating throats raw
because we damn well can and
no one's gonna be on time to work in the morning anyway, woo hoo!

When I was a kid, I didn't dream about writing
poems; I wanted to play I-back for the Huskers.
Now I'm a lot older, more experienced;
and I still have four years of eligibility left.

The Funny Poet Renounces Funny Poetry And Concentrates On Making The World A Better, More Beautiful Place (In Which He Has Sex More Often)

The everlasting universe of things
Flows through the mind, and rolls its rapid waves,
Now dark—now glittering—now reflecting gloom—
Now lending splendor....

—from "Mont Blanc" by Percy Bysshe Shelley

I do try to write poems that make you want to feed someone a sandwich, rescue orphans, fight a revolution, write a strong note of protest to the President or surprise me with a kiss. Long metaphors rich in the foliage of the Nishnabotna River Valley, as open as the sky above these plains.

And I cough up donuts and cows. Little Debbie blowing the Doughboy. Sanskrit chimichanga recipes. It happens.

I couldn't believe when a local news station put me on TV for three minutes to talk up National Poetry Month, and I read a touching poem about spiced pork rinds, and when I got home to watch it on the VCR, found I spent the interview with "FUNNY POET" typed under my face; and I like being funny, it's a compliment, but chrissakes, not always the compliment I'm fishing for, sometimes I want to be dangerous, sensitive. Like Shelley.

So no more cows. I'll write about Harleys and willow trees now; I never want to drive up to the mall, park under the sign "Today Only: Sock Puppets And Funny Poet," so goodbye cows.

Well, one more. I still haven't written Brenda, the escaped Australian cow running free for nine months until helicopters and night vision goggles and, come on, one more and that's it, no more pork rinds, no more Graceland trips or Marlin Perkins, just mountains struggled over, Salvadoran freedom fighters, your breasts like hyacinths.

When young, I wanted to be Percy Bysshe Shelley, Kermit the Frog, and Roger Rabbit. I mean:

> "And the sunlight clasps the earth
> And the moonbeams kiss the sea:
> What is all this sweet work worth
>   If thou kiss not me?" [1]

and who doesn't want to make "millions of people happy" like Kermit or hear the justification for love, "He makes me laugh," spoken by a Jessica Rabbit: words from a cartoonist's dream sliding through the lips those dreams drew. And not that I was jacking off to some bright Barbie with implants, it was the words saying that laughter superceded muscletone, even posture, that funny was somehow powerful.

But it just means you're not taken seriously. You're the Moon Pie on the dessert tray of the black tie dinner at that snooty French restaurant. You're the guy who hurls on the Jamaican ambassador during the White House luncheon, you've got the fake arrow through your head as the Poet Laureate floats past in a smog of tweed, you're....

What?

What are you looking at me like that for?

What?

[1] Untitled fragment by Percy Bysshe Shelley.

Right now, I'm not talking
about dictatorships, about making Patagonia boots
for a dollar a day, about pineapple
sweeter than life, about electricity
and water supplied as luxuries:

I'm talking about chickens.

Roosters on the cartoons always sat silent like
nature's alarm clock
until the sun sprang over the horizon and the dark
shot away like a window shade flapping.

Just another childhood lie;

as cocks don't just perform at 5:58a.m., then take the day and night off, they
          stay up
all night, shouting:
"HEY HEY HEY HEY HEY, WHAT'S UP?" and another
starts in about hamburger prices followed
by a few more using every square centimeter of lung to argue
about the elections in May, and the real problem

is that everyone here has chickens,

all your neighbors, all their neighbors, chickens
under your window, under the floorboards,
locked in closets, inside the plumbing, behind the walls,
stuffed in the mattresses, in the pockets of your pants set out for tomorrow.

And at night,

you've brushed your teeth, you look outside
at a brilliantly starry silent sky. Then you yawn
and somehow wake one up
and within seconds the world is crowing,
every constellation is yelling, every

fricking chicken in the universe is out there tonight
shouting "NO NO NO NO NO,
listen to ME! listen to ME!"

Science And Love: Lines Composed After Reading an Article About How Love May be Triggered by Scents

Maybe the scientists are right, maybe it is just chemical, just pheremones,
light refraction, DNA, tactile impact, circumstantial scents
releasing the balloons and banners in our blood,
the trumpets in our heartbeat, the cheering throng of every pore and follicle.
I can see it

as I've tried to be in love before with precise women:
faces and attitudes ripe for sonnets, all
I could ask for if I were to write out my wishes to Santa or Cupid
or whoever manufactures these things;
though now, I suppose, it could be science,

could be Microsoft or Dow or US Steel or Beatrice,
maybe my fascination with Little Debbie isn't so absurd,
maybe that factory can
box me some love
as long as they get the scent correct.

I only say this
because I am in love
and not with anyone like the description on my Christmas list;
I mean,
she's an English major,

she's blond,
she loves brussel sprouts, doesn't have a car, still lives with her parents.
She must just smell OK.
That'd make sense.
There must be an algebraic equation

to graph how the grey of her eyes can make me lose whole
sentences already set in motion;
a chart surely shows
how a precise tilt of her head and vocal inflection can make me need
to touch the skin curving over her shoulder;

and when my lips parabola up
at her voice on the phone;
it's pitch and timbre playing my lizard brain like an accordion and
my stomach's sack of nerves
like a dulcimer.

Hippocrates, you old bearded Greek,
how does it feel to be so close to Venus?
Einstein, Hawking, Oppenheimer:
you could've been Garbo and Marilyn combined
if you'd looked to these little endocrines instead;

but no matter,
I'm seeing her tonight
and all I need to know
is up my nose
where there are candelabra and fireplaces waiting

for her
to come close
and ignite.

After The Strategic Air Command

And what's to notice?
In summers home from college, I'd drive
to the SAC Museum and pick her up for a date.

In a scene like that, how can
machines across the globe be watching,
pointing at you, ready

to flick your city like a matchstick?
We didn't run in hot panic,
like wax down candles, past

the Dakota missile warrens
to some divot in the planet that no
computer anywhere cared about, we went to

Dairy Queen, talked
as the sunset washed away another blue sky.
Air Force men under the ground

were as real as trolls to us then.
And now the SAC really is
gone, even its museum bombers

carted down rural roads to a new site west of here.
And you can imagine what you will,
no one's cracked

this planet like an egg in a truckstop kitchen,
we sit safe
in our churches, safe in our homes

eating solid breakfasts
in small bites.

And in the South Bay, it's
surrounded by them,
by FMC, Lockheed, Varian, Martin Marietta, Watkins Johnson,
and more, more, more
people making tanks, making missiles, making lug nuts and computer
        guidance chips
for atomic warheads,
parts of bombers and F-16s, land mines, rockets, everything
a modern military covets.
Even flimsy fallbacks like the rifle,
even that.

And in the middle there, across
from the shopping center, next to the theater complex
is the madwoman's curse,
this obsession from pioneer eccentricity.

With Dad off work for the weekend, families pay
and tour the stairways to nowhere,
doors to brick walls, the thirteen bathrooms,
ghost-driven sprawl
cracking and spiraling for fear
of all those killed by her husband's creation,
"the gun that won
the west" fattening the skies with these angry dead,

more souls
at more
doors every day,
watching her,
thirsty
for that
flicker
at her neck,
waiting
for the hammers

to pause
as only then
can they can rip
her apart

since her
money is their
blood, her fortune
flowing from the wounds of those at the wrong end
of a Winchester,
from the arms and legs, hearts and lungs and kidneys,
guts and eyes burst apart, splintered
skulls, all of it.

And the minivans gush from the surrounding communities,
children dashing up
another staircase to a ceiling. They think
what a queer old gal she
must've been
and laugh
as they cross
the parking lot
under a sky
that swells
with roiling clouds.

Oh, this Old World spangle hanging
off the window frames and gutters, the colored lights
and glass, bronze, and brass and silver, white
lace shapes playing hide and seek in the trees,
holiday songs slapping passersby
on the strip mall sidewalks with the ice
and salt and gravel, fire under purse-pockets,
hearts fluttering at the possibility of free gift wrapping.

Open me up, angel, fill me like
a red stocking with cookies and bangles, candy
canes, bows, cards, anything red
or green or snowflake-shaped, pluck me a bright star or
a savior I can fit in my pocket,
beat the drums in Christmas rhythms, dance
to the Salvation Army bell, and flail, for this
fire commands us rejoice! rejoice!

And whether you're in Orlando or Denver or Seattle or Des Moines,
this is winter, this is short on daylight,
long on night, bright darkness holding
us like ropes hold the mast holding the sail
stretched wide, holds us like a sale
on the sweater that we need most.

Hold me like the cream
holds the oatmeal,
like the fig grips the bar,
like the jelly holds

onto the roll. These flavors,
impermanent but inseparable,
joined for life
conceivably beyond

expiration dates and shelf-lives,
never know they grow old; they never
pass into that darkest maw
alone.

To walk into the hangar, step
after step along one of these steel
whales, I feel chilled.

Don't mistake me, I appreciate this
abstract scattering of technology but am not proud
of it, of B-36s, FB111s, SR71s,

alphabets and mathematics combined to spell,
to add, to subtract, to write Histories,
to divide.

I apologize.
I must seem heavy-handed when
well-dressed guests sit across the building,

clapping as the orchestra plays *Slow
Dancing In The Living Room,* as waiters weave
sharply through the course

of red, white, and blue tables,
in a more polite evening
of pomp and tablecloths.

And I put my hand
on the husk
of a hydrogen bomb

set out for families
to pass by
and pretend they can grasp.

And if we stood
smaller than the overlapping lambda clones, we'd be
awestruck by the DNA dot blots as big as the moon.

Oh, our white coats
would fit us wrong in such robust environs,
we'd have to put on boots and wide-crowned hats,

considering ourselves kings
of infinite space, though enclosed
in a gnotobiotic mouse gut.

We would lasso and break wild
facultative anaerobes and ride those proud beasties
through the valleys and scrub and conventional Northern blot analysis,

then sleep under that darkest sky
as synthetic oligonucleotides howl
over the horizon that we'll strike for

come the morning,
heading out to see
what happens downstream.

I can't fall asleep at night with her in my head;
   no, it's not fantastic, pornographic, or even romantic,
   just her name,
just the shadows draping off of her
as if she sat across the room near the edge of that moonlight whisper.
I don't really even picture her,
   as if I can't look at her directly,
   as if I'm too polite or shy to;
but she has a cathedral in her name bulging from my blind spot.

You see, I could read by her,
   she conducts through my wiring, she saturates the air
    like radio signals, exists as neither particle nor wave,
she is the gravity that ties me
   to this world and the tide that pulls me away;
    I could breathe only her.

Another

One way to start
is to admit I believe that aliens built the Pyramids, Stonehenge,
and most of my ex-girlfriends, another

is to weep for what's broken, day to day, broken
as if we lay cheek to concrete, grabbing at pennies and wishing
for pillows, for sheets besides the sheets of rain.

This story, like all stories, is a fantasy
about waking up in love on a bright day where sandwiches are emancipated,
given free to idealists and dreamers.

From here, the sliver of your leg
between thin, red skirt and black boot
is the wrong calf to worship,

this barely-even fantasy on this street
where bulldozers bob in drumbeats,
brown cars pull politely around me. I move,

more precisely, I stay still
as if the streetlights won't click on tonight,
as if the sun won't show its face again ever.

But there's always a tomorrow, it's only a day away:
that's the worst of it, breaking in
on what we can gather from sleep

without ever having the proper hands to keep hold of.
And the streetlights do shove their heads
up through the dusk, and I lose interest in the goings on,

keep my feet to back streets,
knowing there's purpose in purpose,
that instinct blurs our judgment into an optimism

stronger than Zoloft or Prozac
so that we might still sleep
beneath God, might consider ourselves lovely.

Wound, 9/13/01

I heard an airplane overhead for the first time
since Tuesday. I ran outside like a dog would,
watched it chase away, fade into clouds.

On AM radio, we want eyes, we want teeth;
on television, we want comprehension,
numbers, definitions, camera angles

as we wait
to understand past and future only,
since we are lacking anything present, current, now.

Our flag is a diversity of patterns,
we work it into metaphors explaining
"We will not tolerate terrorism"

as if we daily once did. You don't fix broken arms
with utility saws, and you don't stand still when a car turns toward you;
it's good we have no now, no current, no present.

Revenge. Zealotry. Limbs for limbs for
funded them, trained them, gave them weapons to fight Communism.
Our anthem will play at Buckingham Palace for the first time.

Another plane rises past, birds scatter,
one thumps against my window and maneuvers crookedly.
A flag is a diversity

of symbols and colors
made as one cloth.
A bandage, a loved one, this moment.

Have you ever been in the situation where you felt that you needed to write
the poem of your life? Scrap together everything
you've ever learned so you can earn her love again?

It's these times you realize how costly it is,
it's these times you wish you'd stayed in school
or, instead of poetry, had studied a science with its soothing rationality.

Have you ever had the fear that the poem of your life is being written
somewhere else by some hack who used to script for *As The World Turns,*
some marketing pimp whose career highlight is a Jensen Tires ad,

that a newspaper columnist named "Moonbeam" is right now poised above a
        page, ready
to strike, to rhyme *Love* and *Dove* and *Glove*
in the climactic stanza in the poem of your life?

And the poem of your life, you know you've felt
the rhythm before, but how does it start?
You know it ends in some shade of brilliance,

that you ease all listeners from an unexpected laughter
into tears for all elusive beauty in this beautiful world.
But how does it go, again?

Have you ever realized that the poem of your life is bottled
in a pen, and that the pen with the poem of your life inside it
is laced in the fingers of a woman

whose love you once dropped?
Whether it's a memo, a credit card receipt or a shopping list,
you don't even breathe when she might be writing.

A car leaves Omaha, moving away from you.
If it averages 71 miles per hour, when will it get to Lincoln?
If the car arrives in Kearney in 170 minutes,
North Platte in 261, if it hits Ogalala in under 300 minutes,
does that indicate this is your fault?

At what point will you stop staring West?
What time does the sun set
assuming she gets to Cheyenne at 5:43 Mountain Time?

It's a shame you can't use calculus,
algebra, or trig in a situation like this,
as they're all so handy on the problems
in the book, every one can be solved,
nobody calls anything "Impossible,"
the worst it can be is "Not solved yet."

And you want to calculate the volume of a feeling
suddenly multiplied by negative one,
want to get to the square root,
find the angle that keeps her happy,
not sit calculating pain to the last digit.

None of this adds, doesn't even subtract, only divides,
divides as if on a calculator where that's the only function,
no X, no plus sign or minus, no equals

just That greater than This
where This is a fraction, the graph of a line
diving off the grid, and That is equal
to an imaginary number I thought was my life.

If a man thinks about a woman at 2 a.m. Central Standard, and he paces his
        apartment at 2 miles per hour,
at what point does he reach,
at what point does he realize?

Saga of the Done-Wrong Open Mic Love Poem

When I gave her nothing, it was more than enough;
and when I gave her everything, she forgot it
in the ashtray at a pancake house.
Oh, I know you've heard this poem, be it soulsong or shitstorm
that someone right now is reading their version of
in an open mic in Portland and Muncie,
in a Barnes & Noble in Manhattan, a Grand Forks coffee bar; this very second
this very poem is being written in Winnipeg and Albuquerque,
is being translated into Spanish, Mandarin, and Bombara,
opened up across the globe as the taste of her
or him sours in our mouths,
but the loss of her grows sweeter
than a donut, than kulfi, than Coca-Cola, guarana,
an apple, two oranges, a freshly peeled kiwifruit.
It's horrifying, all this loss, as if the universal language isn't just music
but a done-wrong Country/Western ballad,
a torch song, a requiem, the blues;
all of us lamenting
that when God shuts a door, He opens
a vein; that there are thousands of fish in the sea,
but I still live landlocked in Nebraska.
The Tower of Babel is erased,
we all have this common language,
this emotional Esperanto which no one can hear
over the coffee grinder, but everyone applauds anyway
because some souls do right, some souls recognize
this taproot, this pain, this love
served steaming, with cream, two sugars,
definitely not decaf, too hot to drink down,
best sipped slow
so it can cool.

And the moon coming up over Cozad
looks too big to be moon,
like a bad-special-effect movie moon
eight times too big and stretched
too thin over blue.
My car shadow is drawn a mile
over corn stubble, pointing
straight at that white mouth
which pulls me between Ahab and Jonah,
swallowed in denials and obsessions as I rise
inside it, as I push myself
into flamingo wisps.
In two weeks, there'll be nothing to see;
in two more, it'll bloom again,
it'll take its chances in this wilderness,
rise bright across the east
and shrink like old desires
as it lights the way away.

Tell the good news about Jesus

—a bumper sticker I followed for a long time

Jesus lent me ten bucks when I forgot my wallet at lunch.
Sure, he could've ordered a chicken pesto sandwich
and broke it into two full meals, but he's no showoff.
That's what I like about Jesus.

Jesus listens to cool music. If it weren't for Jesus,
I never would have known about Tom Waits
or Ani DiFranco, and I sure wouldn't own any Lyle Lovett CDs.
But Jesus makes a kickass mix tape.

Jesus loves cows,
thinks my poems with cows in them are a hoot
and encourages me
to look at herds of white cows
in a green field
and imagine salvation
is underneath each windmill.

Jesus tells me Pat Robertson's right,
and so is Al Sharpton.
That they're both wrong, too,
but that's not the point.
His point is how God is sewn into every fabric.
Even yourself. Even Elvis.

Jesus saves and Jesus recycles.

Jesus eats fish for more
than Omega-3 fatty acids,
drinks red wine for more reasons
than his sacred heart.

Jesus doesn't dress like the Medieval paintings
with the gold hats and the Mr. T rosaries.
Sure, he can clean up nice,
but Jesus likes blue jeans.
Jesus makes a killer chianti,
but he refuses to turn water
into Diet Coke for me.
"What's the difference?" he asks.

Jesus pisses me off
with his honesty
sometimes.
But it's not like he's ever wrong.

Jesus acts real serious
when somebody rushes up to him hollering, "Jesus,
take me up to Heaven,
I will see you in the Kingdom, Jesus!"
Jesus says they should get their kumbayayas off
by putting on some overalls
and hammering in the morning:
may as well make Heaven bigger,
not just your ego.

Jesus digs the "How does Jesus eat M&M's" joke.
He won't do it at a party, but he did do it once
when just the two of us were watching cartoons.

Jesus wanted me to tell you he loves you.
Jesus also wants you to stop doing that thing.

Jesus tells me I'm saved.
Then he laughs real loud.
I hate it when Jesus does that.

Storytellers love to recite
passages from *The Arabian Nights:*
in it, a man marries a new bride
every day,
              that is to say
after his henchmen
have opened the previous night's bride like a book
and read her into the sand.
Storytellers love this

because a bride finally comes along
and tells stories that keep her blood
inside the margins,
a new story every night
for a thousand and one nights
keeps her pages bound to her spine,
her biography open-ended,
the sinews and the bones of her neck
safe from blow
after blow
after blow of a blunt blade's staccato.

Storytellers don't usually stress that part.
How much it actually takes
to saw through the cords knotted into a neck,
the ways blood bursts out of body,
surprisingly different for each different girl.

The storytellers don't refer so much to the other wives:
the dancer who lasted three nights
then didn't have another dance and needed more than wine on that short
          fourth night;
or the painter who almost saw a second night;
or the laundrywoman made royal for a day, lifespan
of a butterfly, knowing you don't survive a thousand and one nights
doing a thousand and one loads of laundry,
no matter how useful that is;

66

beautiful faces
with desert as dowry,
beautiful bodies, beautiful bodies, hundreds
of bodies, naked trenches spilling

while one tongue
breaks off stories
word by word
to feed a king.

Imagine that:
your life hangs
on a thread,
a spice, a syllable,
survives on pages—But

do you believe it's just coincidence
it's the storyteller who survives the story?
Do you ever imagine how our fables would end if it were the washerwomen
who recorded our histories,
imagine our fairy tales
when Cinderella doesn't need a pumpkin,
doesn't need Walt Disney,
doesn't need magic, doesn't need fairies,

she only needs
her soaps,
her wits,
her wrists.

The morning broke like rope hoisting a piano in that scene you only see in
      movies, four stories over the street to crash over one soul jolted by the
      clock radio clicking on with a Def
      Leppard song you never cared if you heard again,
certainly not now,
as morning spills all over your bed,
this shattered fishbowl casting you over the sheets,
gasping.

I. Nogales

It's not like driving to Winnipeg
where you change nations easy as a shirt.
You leave your car parked
on a street whose name you tattoo to your fears,
that you look back for every time
you hear metal strike concrete;
as this is not the same
as the sidewalks and Mexican restaurants of your land
with its street lights and trash cans:
this is the neighbor at the weed-grown dead end
who you wish would either mow his lawn or get evicted,

this is bodies
in the streets
selling cotton candy and Robert Goulet CDs
to the clot of autos inching back toward the border,
man with a styrofoam cup and a stump
where his pantleg flaps;
there's no Texaco or Applebees here, señor,
none of the chain stores you say you hate, no familiar sights

except for human faces
which seem out of place
in this architecture, which remind you nothing
of comfort.
          Oh, how you've been lied to.
You stand on a corner yourself now, blinking your eyes,
with nothing in your mouth to tell the world
but lies.

II. Arizona

A night clear enough
to see for universes
out above the headlight constellations.
The moon in profile
lies across the landscape
in patterns like shadows.

Driving so long,
you wear the car like clothing.
Grey dust of another country on your boots,
dust of worlds and cosmos
cut across your lips.
Monument rocks are out there,

subtle against black everythingness
painted underneath the galaxies.
What Tucson and Phoenix and Flagstaff,
what Florence and Camp Verde and Cameron break,
the miles carefully craft back into shape
with tools smaller than hands and pins and toothpicks.

You can see breath on the windshield,
the invisible coming visible, space
we think of as empty
that watches us
carefully
like tiger eyes bundled in the canopy:

these things that stir
and are.

III. The Grand Canyon

The Canyon, people say, is a wonder, a wonder
of the natural world, one river's dream
pulled grain by grain from the earth,
teaching us to gasp. My eyes, like ravens,

sweep over sand and tumbleweed, past
open-front shanties where there'll be authentic sorts
of crafted bracelets for sale at dawn.

But these ravens pull further,
across smooth hill and desert forest,
clawing toward that cliff lip,

famished for its beauty
coming up

across the horizon.

> *There are known knowns. These are things we know that we know. There are known unknowns. That is to say, there are things that we know we don't know. But there are also unknown unknowns. There are things we don't know we don't know.*
>
> —Secretary of Defense Donald Rumsfeld clarifying US policy on the war on terror at a Department of Defense news briefing

It
  's not always
      the little boy
who cries
        Wolf!
                   sometimes
the wolf
cries
wolf

    and
        points   away.

Duct tape your doors shut,
we're on Code Orange, Code Orange, people,
blue skies
        no matter, there's anthrax
somewhere, somebody said something about smallpox
   wherever, an unnamed man reportedly said something
            big
was coming down
  eventually. A man said
people were going to die,
people are going to die,
Americans are going to die.

Officials are quoted as saying
things, officials are quoted as saying, *Hurry, hurry, run,*
seal yourself in a Ziploc bag
in a lead-walled box
in a hole
in the earth
in prayer to our God,

and sources report
we aren't ready, we're not scared enough
and if we
don't get a little more hysterical,
then it's the terrorists who will win

because sources suggest
it could be any day, hour, minute, second–
         duck!
it could be any metropolis, city, small town, farmstead,
or possibly somewhere else; for God's sake,
there are
       experts
            saying
We're not safe, we're not safe,
now do what we say

and nobody gets hurt.

There's fear
out past your walls, there's fear itself
blowing against the plastic sheeting and the bars of grey tape,
there's so much
to fear, we must do more,
we have to fight them,
kill them, cripple them
for Jesus,
      Amen!

It's not always
        the little boy
        who cries
          Wolf!

Sometimes the wolf
      cries wolf.

And it's not always the wolf
our little boys are sent out
to kill.

How I Love You (the John Ashcroft Remix)

To those who scare peace-loving people with phantoms of lost liberty, my message is this: Your tactics only aid terrorists, for they erode ournational unity and diminish our resolve.

—Attorney General John Ashcroft

Yes, it's true:
I have been taking pictures of you
with a camera hidden in the blue bag I claim to carry for my diabetes.
I'm not diabetic.
I have accepted John Ashcroft as my personal savior.

See, I come out to your poetry readings
and memorize the poems you read,
then write them down
in braille, then photograph the transcript,
then burn the film, then eat the paper, then send the stool sample to the
        Department of Homeland Security

because I
have accepted John Ashcroft
as my personal savior.

I collect other stool samples, too,
but am not cleared to go into that right now because I
have accepted John Ashcroft as my personal savior.

That's why I invite you to my parties
where I collect the beer bottles you guzzle from.
                        No,
not for anything as pedestrian as fingerprints or saliva samples;
we collected your prints and fluids years ago
off the CIA operatives you still think was just some "crazy ex-girl or
        boyfriend."

No, I collect them for your brain waves embedded in the glass.
And because they're recyclable.
And because I have accepted John Ashcroft as my personal savior.

I hope you understand,
I've tapped your phones and spatulas
because I love you,

put carpet samples up my ass
and sent subliminal commands through the thousands of emails you think
        are only about Russian brides, mortgages, and farm teens gone bad
because I
am a patriot;

I have done all of this
for your good,
my good,
Omaha's good,
America's good:
for Apple and IBM, for J. Lo and Ben,
Barbie and Ken, *Survivor* and *Friends,*
for Al Gore and sex
                among consenting married heterosexual adult
women and men

because I have accepted
John Ashcroft as
my personal savior.

And don't be scared, I'm
not here to take your apartment
or employment or retirement away, that's not
my job. My job
is just to keep you laughing, keep you listening
to the funny poem
so you won't stray too much,
pay too much attention to that stream-of-consciousness ramble some
other poet's reading: that
sloppy poem, that overuses-the-word-"revolution"-too-much poem, that
heartfelt poem, cast-your-vote-with-a-stone poem,

that register-your-sad-ass-to-actually-vote poem,
that get-out-of-bed-on-election-day, put-down-the-gordita-and-actually-go-
        to-a-polling-place-and-vote poem,
because
I
have accepted John Ashcroft
as my personal
savior.

Melodrama Of A Poet Watching The Sky For Storms

I kissed Matt Mason and all I got was this lousy plaque.

—from a plaque in a dream by Sarah Mckinstry-Brown

There are matters
of geography and time aligned brighter
than stars against us,
rather than us
pressed against us. There are busses that insist
on leaving this town.
So many locomotives
skimming like longships across iced cornfields,

and I remember losing my fingers
in the coils of your hair.
I remember losing
my breath
with every step back
to my car—so early in the morning, or too late
in the night, where the snowflakes brush me
like feathers from dark swans.

Because when a train leaves a town,
those silver tibias and fibulas curl and crawl;
when a train leaves a town,
those bones rotate
as if they carry a weight
heavier than this town that I love.
I only say this because it is supposed to be tragic.

Surprisingly, the skies do lighten
behind ivory screens, a soft glow
that falls in swirls
of snow. It's beautiful,

really. I could open my mouth,
my tongue curved up
until I drink this whole sky
back to blue. Because, you see, when I get back
to my place, my bedroom doesn't echo
like I expected it would.
It sighs like a sleepy dog, it still breathes
with the scent you dabbed on last night.

But this is supposed to be dramatic,
please pardon my distraction:
you showed up seven days ago
and colored my days
like the bur oaks and hickories soon will
with green-flecked brown disguised
as your eyes, touches
as awkward as starlight
grown hastily into constellations
that some sailors steer by,
that some scientists study; and I
open my mouth to,
my tongue curved up,
drinking down this sky
because it is not bitter
and because it is my heart.

In spring, I fall in love with redbud trees,
take the city off like a jacket
and walk into the hawthorns and hickories,

red oaks and black walnuts showing here in a brown and white movie.
Except for a mist of new color on them.
I'll call this green, though it's so much

brighter, moving in a fog across the ground,
in the air, in the voices of birds returning,
in the swelling of temperatures

to come. The tree trunks blur
into branches and river bluffs,
wash each others' distinctions away

though the police siren and the jet engine and the interstate hum
from out there
call "Ahem. Ahem!" to any reverie that may be budding.

In spring, I walk through warm, green breath,
past shagbark and basswood, past saplings and towers,
to the whisperers, the stubble growing out

in shades of lavender, in the shy gasps of color I come here for,
that I've watched every face around me for,
closed my eyes and inhaled for,

waiting to know the touch
of this,
which, in spring, I fall in love with

and spend the rest of the seasons searching for,
for the home these colors commute from,
the street, the apartment number, the door.

Saying Goodbye Again At The Amtrak Station, 6:15 AM

Before we define ourselves
into the little plastic figures
on top of a cake,
before we define ourselves
into broken keys and bitter poetry,
into any theoretical,
maybe we needed to have
a real first date first; or,
if not that, a second
chance. I drop you off awkwardly, kiss you
goodnight before your house
takes its front door east across fields,
opening over the Missouri, the Mississippi,
Great Lakes, Appalachia, Adirondacks.
I imagine you standing
with the aurora borealis now,
like colors out of fables that we tell over campfires
and wish for. In my dreams, light bends through you
as you flare against the sky, exciting
the atoms
of night.

Inside the restaurant in the indifferent city,
our cheeks are sanded red
by the gusts off the lake
that tumbled us with winds of fears,
which crouched
picking their teeth
with the bones of our hopes.
Some days, see,
I feel like I can explain.
Some days, see, I know
how to be smooth,
and some days my smooth
is pretty chunky. But today,

I may be earth by vocation,
but I am avalanche by air,
pushing through the atmosphere
with the subtlety of fire.

Prosciutto curls like bacon
when you cook it. Just a touch
more purple.

You are more beautiful
than bacon,
than salmon, than feta, than Stilton.

Hersheys, Cadburys, Toblerones melt
in your light. Even M&Ms blush
at your touch.

When you sit down,
the best steaks realize
they're slivers

chipped from cow,
tortes and ambrosias remember
they're only tinted sugar.

You see, I've spent years
casing menus for your touch,
searching under grocery store fluorescents;

I've shrunk so thin,
I can only hold a measured shock,
the lemon water of small kisses

building me back
from bones to flesh,
smoke to mountain to sky.

Love has spent thirty-one nights on this futon.
Love reads herself to bleariness, laughing and napping,
shakes herself early to rise for work,
wakes him with a kiss, tells him the dreams
she's walked, warming his skin along the shore of her touch:
  her flesh the ocean
      that only dreamers dream to look across,
    that only dreamers ask
   what's on the other side
  of these blue sheets.

          We say adventurers like this
are daring; maybe they just have too much free time
to wonder; maybe they're only autistic romantics.
                    But

for thirty-one nights,
he has charted by lamplight,
dreamed of round continents,
civilizations and history books.
For thirty-one nights,
he prayed beyond Sinbad
or Columbus or Ulysses or any myth of the seas;
so what thrill, what discovery on this thirty-second night

                    to come upon the very edge
                          of all there is
                           and to fall

                            from

                           sight.

Every morning you'd think
all the moths would throw themselves
into the Sun.

But they wait
for streetlights
to consume them

in small coughs
of sparkle.
My dear,

my dear,
my dear:
I have stopped

listening to my moth soul.
My dear, I am done
tilting at streetlights.

My paper wings soar,
brush
your blazing heart.

I. Sandias

The name for these mountains translates
as "watermelon" despite how they open
over tan landscapes and cactus. Human bodies,
whatever climate, are a certain percent
water. Except for you. You are a marvel
born here like a river sprung from rock,
freshwater tumult which would fill other skins
to bursting.

II. The Desert Rose

When lightning throws its heavenly weight against the desert,
the ground holds, but its sand skin blooms
in roses. And with centuries of storms in this oven,
the horizons hold
an ocean of boulder fleck, rock seed,
sun-packed dust swimming with punctuation marks
shocked into blossom.

And when your toes
struck the faded farmland here,
when your fingers thundered across my husk:
alfalfa sprouted in rivers of daisies, honey
burst from cornstalks, acres flooded
into flower, my voice burst
into rain.

After earning his MA in Creative Writing from the University of California at
Davis, Matt Mason, of course, moved to Omaha where he now lives with his
wonderful wife Sarah and baby daughter Sophia. There, he edits
PoetryMenu.com, a listing of every Nebraska poetry event (and, yes, there are
a lot, see for yourself) and founded Morpo Press which, since 1997, has
published 25 chapbooks by up-and-coming local writers. He also runs the
Omaha Healing Arts Center Poetry Slam (on the 2nd Saturday of every
month, drop by and say "Hello") as well as the occasional reading series. Over
100 magazines and anthologies have published his poems, including *Laurel
Review, Prairie Schooner, The Morpo Review*, and *Mississippi Review* (online
edition). New Michigan Press released his chapbook *Mistranslating Neruda* in
2003; not to be outdone, Lone Willow Press put out *When The Bough Breaks*
in 2005. Matt has read his poetry everywhere from behind the podiums of the
Nebraska Book Festival to the stages of the National Poetry Slam as well as at
universities, high schools, libraries, book stores, radio shows, state fairs, art
museums, bars, ice cream parlors, and coffee shops across the country, even
appearing as the stand-in for Poet Laureate Ted Kooser and Oscar-winning
director Alexander Payne at rehearsals for the opening of a performing arts
center. He was appointed an Admiral in the Great Navy of the State of
Nebraska by Governor Mike Johanns in 2004, enjoys donuts and sometimes
does write about cows. Mason has a spiffywebsite at MidVerse.com.

Printed in the United States
86188LV00001B